William Henry Hadow

A Croatian Composer

Notes Toward the Study of Joseph Haydn

William Henry Hadow

A Croatian Composer
Notes Toward the Study of Joseph Haydn

ISBN/EAN: 9783744678971

Printed in Europe, USA, Canada, Australia, Japan

Cover: Foto ©Thomas Meinert / pixelio.de

More available books at **www.hansebooks.com**

A CROATIAN COMPOSER

NOTES TOWARD THE STUDY

OF

JOSEPH HAYDN

BY

W. H. HADOW, M.A.

Fellow of Worcester College, Oxford
Author of "Studies in Modern Music"

LONDON
SEELEY AND CO. LIMITED
38 GREAT RUSSELL STREE
1897

TO

W. R. MORFILL

*A small return for much assistance
and encouragement*

PREFACE.

THE materials for this essay have been almost entirely gathered from two works by Dr. František Š. Kuhač, the one his collection of South-Slavonic Folksongs, the other a pamphlet upon Joseph Haydn. Indeed, so greatly am I indebted to them that the essay would not have been written had it been possible to present them to the reader more directly. All that has been added is a certain re-arrangement of the data, a certain amount of commentary and exposition, and a few supplementary facts which happen to have come within my reach. I should state that during a recent visit to Croatia, I saw Dr. Kuhač, who most kindly gave me full permission to make use of his results, and augmented the gift with much valuable information.

It is not for me to determine how far the subject will be of interest to English readers. We have somewhat forgotten Haydn: we do not always attach great importance to abstract problems. But I venture to think that the practical issue is not insignificant, and that in any case the question of historical truth is one which demands some consideration and regard. There is little need to say that I am myself convinced of the point which I have endeavoured to make: if the facts have been misinterpreted, at least the endeavour may invite discussion.

No doubt it will have to take its chance with those critics who would censure it at the outset for prying too curiously behind the veil. From such antagonists I beg, for two reasons, courteously to differ. In the first place, this is not a question of irrelevant detail, but an inquiry into the methods of a great artist, and into the character of his work. Grant that it deals with a single aspect alone, it does not therefore disregard or undervalue the others. And to suppose that Haydn is depreciated by the acknowledgment of his debt to his age and country is, I think, somewhat to misunderstand the conditions under which all true " creative " art is produced. In the second place, if we accept the historical statement as true, we do something to rescue a musical nation from undeserved neglect. The race which has given to a master not only birth but inspiration may surely claim from us something better than the oblivion into which we have allowed its name to fall.

I wish to offer all due acknowledgment to Mr. L. Finkenstein for his translation of Dr. Kuhač's pamphlet.

OXFORD, *October* 12, 1897.

A CROATIAN COMPOSER.

THE study of Human Nature contains few problems more difficult or more important than those which deal with distinctions of national character. In most countries the original race, itself not always pure, has been affected and modified by a hundred causes; by conquest, by immigration, by intermarriage with neighbours, by all the circumstances and conditions of historical development; and the result is commonly a web of many diverse threads, in which we are fortunate if we can explain the prevailing colour and the prevailing pattern. Sometimes, as in our Indian Empire, the threads lie comparatively free, and puzzle us more by their number and variety than by actual closeness of texture. Sometimes, as in the Kingdom of Hungary, the interplay is so thorough and so complex as almost to baffle analysis at the outset. And when to this is added the influence of climate, of government, of religion, of all that is implied in past record and traditional usage, it will be seen that the question of causality is one which may well tax to their utmost limit the skill and patience of the ethnologist.

But if the reasons are hard to trace, the fact is no longer open to intelligible doubt. Physiology tells us that it manifests itself at birth; history, that it has formed a channel for the whole course and current of events. There is no crisis so great, there is no occurrence so trivial, as not to exhibit in some degree its presence and efficacy in the life of man. Nations at peace do not follow the same policy; nations in conflict do not fight with the same weapons; the contrast of laws and customs is so vivid that it has led some impatient philosophers to consider all morality relative. And what is true of the life as a whole is equally true of its specialisation in art and literature. For these are pre-eminently the expression of the national voice, as intimate as its language, as vital as the breath that it draws, and every artist who has compelled the attention of the world at large has done so by addressing it as the spokesman of his own people.

No doubt there are other factors in the case, the personal idiosyncrasy that separates a man from his fellows, and again the general principles, fewer perhaps than is commonly supposed, that underlie all sense of rhythm and all appreciation of style. But to say this is only to say that the artist is himself, and that he belongs to our common humanity. In everything, from the conception of a poem to the structure of a sentence, the national element bears its part with the other two; it colours the personal temperament, it gives a standpoint from which principles of style are approached, and wherever its influence is faint or inconsiderable the work of the artist will be found to suffer in proportion. It is hardly necessary to add that the law holds equally good whether the race in question be pure or mixed. If the former, it will move along a single line : if the latter, it will mark the converging point of many ; but in either case its operation is a sure test of genuineness both in feeling and expression. Occasionally, it may be, a careless public has been deceived by some trick of imitation—by the Spanish comedies of Clara Gazul or the Persian Lyrics of Mirza Schaffy ; but such instances of deception no more traverse the law than the Ireland forgeries or the pictures of Cariani. Some men are born with a talent of mimicry : none have ever by its means attained to greatness.

It may at once be admitted that this rule of national influence is at present less firmly established in music than in poetry or painting. In the two latter arts we have certain obvious externals to aid investigation — broad and salient contrasts of language, wide differences of scene and subject—with which music as such has little or nothing to do. Her subject is usually vague and indeterminate, her vocabulary is made up of a few scales, and for the rest we are told that her genius is limited to the common emotions of mankind and the common inheritance of pure form. But it is wholly false to infer that music is independent of nationality. The composer bears the mark of his race not less surely than the poet or the painter, and there is no music with true blood in its veins and true passion in its heart that has not drawn inspiration from the breast of the mother country.

Two main causes have retarded the acceptance of this truth. First, the belief that national melody is entirely an affair of artifices and mannerisms, that it is constituted by special turns of phrase and figure—as though you could make a rose tree by tying roses to a Scotch fir, or turn "Rule Britannia" into a Hungarian tune by ending it with a Hungarian cadence. This, it may be said, simply misunderstands the nature of the law which it criticises. No doubt a certain range of expression belongs to each type of folksong. No doubt these accidents of figure and phrase appear upon the surface, and are often useful as indications, but it makes all the difference whether they grow naturally in their place or lie there as mere lifeless appendages. Even the foreign idioms which a great composer may occasionally employ are only a graft let into the parent stock; the new growth is at once modified by the influence of the old, and alters its character to match its change of condition. And apart from these rare grafts the phrase of a true master will always be found conformable to the spirit that animates it, not because it constitutes the spirit, but because it emanates as property from essence. The second error springs from our loose and inaccurate methods of classification. That Mozart was an Italian composer seems now to be taken as an accredited jest; but it is more serious when we show our gratitude for the splendid work that Germany has done by scoring to her account all that has been accomplished by her neighbours. Schumann claims Chopin as a fellow-countryman; we are so far from protesting that we add Liszt, for whom "the great German master" was long a newspaper synonym, and even hesitate about Smetana and Dvořák. It is true that classification is often extremely difficult—records are imperfect, names are misleading, histories are marred by want of ethnological knowledge ; but the admission of ignorance is not a very strong basis for dogmatic denial. Critics who traverse a law, because they cannot see its applicability to the facts, would do well to make sure at the outset that the facts have been correctly observed.

The subject of the present essay is one of the most remarkable instances of such misattribution. From the time of Carpani to that of Dr. Nohl, Haydn's biographers have been unanimous in describing him as a German, born, as everybody knows, in Lower Austria, speaking German as his native language, Teutonic in race, in character, in surroundings. Yet the more we study him the more impossible it becomes to regard his music as the work of a Teuton. It is undoubtedly affected by his education and circumstances, by the early study of Emanuel Bach, and the subsequent intercourse with Mozart, but when we penetrate to the essential spirit of the man himself we find that its inherent characteristics are no more German than they are Italian or French. Haydn's sentiment is of a kind without analogue among German Composers—mobile, nervous, sensitive, a little shallow it may be, but as pure and transparent as a mountain stream. His humour is a quality in which he stands almost alone ; it differs totally from the wit of Mozart, or the grim jesting of Beethoven ; it is quaint and playful, rippling over the whole surface of the page, and equally removed from satire and epigram. Again, he has less breadth and stateliness than belong to the German temper, but he has far more versatility. He was the most daring of pioneers, the most hazardous of experimentalists, and, what is more noticeable, his experiments are rather the natural outcome of a restless and vivid imagination than the efforts of a deliberate and conscious reform. From the external side, too, the same contrast is apparent. The shapes of his melodic phrases are not those of the German folksong ; his rhythms are far more numerous and varied; his metres are often strange and unfamiliar. Throughout Western Europe the four-bar line has almost uniformly been taken as the unit of measurement, carrying with it the corresponding stanza of eight or sixteen or thirty-two. In a hundred German or English folksongs it will be strange if a single exception can be found: in a hundred melodies from Haydn's quartets it will be strange if the exceptions are not as frequent as the instances. In a word, his range of stanza is far wider than that known to the Germany of his day, and many of his most characteristic tunes belong to another language and another scheme of versification.

The evidence here briefly epitomised can only point to one of two conclusions: either that the law of nationality is inapplicable to Haydn, or that his assignment to the German race is an ethnological error. The former alternative is unsatisfactory enough; the latter was for many years put out of court by our inability to sustain the *onus probandi*. But in 1878 Dr. Kuhač began to publish his great collection of South-Slavonic melodies,* and in 1880 he supplemented it by a special pamphlet on Haydn's relation to them.† The main points of the thesis are three in number: first, that the Croatian folk-tunes possess all the characteristics which have been noted as distinctive in the melodies of Haydn; second, that many of them are actually employed by him; and third, that the facts of his birth and parentage afford strong presumptive proof that he was a Croatian by race.‡ If this contention can be established it strengthens an important law with valuable and unexpected support, and it remains therefore that we should bring forward a critical statement of the case, beginning, for clearness' sake, with the historical and biographical testimony, and

* Južno-slovjenske Narodne Popievke: Zagreb, 1878-1881.

† Josip Haydn i Hrvatske Narodne Popievke; reprinted from the Vienac, Zagreb, 1880.

‡ As early as 1862 the Lumír put in a claim for Bohemia. This was a step in the right direction, since it represented Haydn as a Slav, but the evidence preponderates in favour of a more Southern origin.

so bringing into prominence the special character of the compositions themselves.

First, then, we must consider whether the character of the Croatian people is such as to render its claim to Haydn reasonable and intelligible. It would be poor logic to illustrate our law by deriving a great artist from an inartistic nation. And the question becomes more pressing when we remember that Haydn's whole family was musical, that he learned his first lessons from his father and mother, that his brother Michael long enjoyed a repute little inferior to his own. But to answer it in the affirmative is to run counter to an established belief. From Mrs. Western in "Tom Jones" to Barto Rizzo in "Vittoria" everybody has had a fling at the Croats. We have come to regard them at best as savages, and at worst as mercenary assassins. The associations that we connect with their name are those of war and pillage, of fierce onslaught and misused victory, of lives bartered for gain or spilled in mere wantonness. Their art is a matter into which we have never dreamed of inquiring, and we should as soon think of learning their language as of accrediting them with a literature. To dispel this superstition it is only needful that we should study the country. Few towns are more charming than Agram, few regions more delightful than the long fertile valley of the Save in which it lies. In the remoter districts there is still much ignorance and much poverty, but civilisation is spreading from the centre, and eliciting, not creating, the signs of progress. The strongest impulse of the national life si loyalty to race and Church. Recent events have shown us that outbreaks may readily be provoked in religious and patriotic causes, but the temper that will fight for them is not ignoble, and is not infrequently conjoined with the inspiration that will make songs in their honour. And throughout the country the love of music prevails.* The men sing at their plough, the girls sing as

* Dr. Kuhač (Josip Haydn, p. 5) declares that one in every three of the population " either sings, plays, or composes." And there is a significant Croatian proverb to the effect that " an age is known by its music."

they fill their water-pots at the fountain; by every village inn you may hear the jingle of the tambura, and watch the dancers footing it on the green. Grant that the music is not always of a high order, that the tunes are often primitive and the voices rude and uncouth, still the impetus is there, and it only needs guidance and direction. Certainly the present condition of the race does not disqualify it to be the parent of a great composer.

It will be objected that this is only a present impression, and that it tells us nothing of those days when, apparently, the whole *raison d'être* of the population was to furnish fighting-men for the army of Maria Theresa. In answer to this, two points must be made clear: first, the state of Croatia proper during the past two centuries; second, the position occupied at the same period by other members of the Croatian race.* The argument "e nihilo nihil" need

* For the sake of clearness, it may be well to say that Croatia proper means that district across the Save of which Agram (*i.e.* Zagreb) is the capital; and that the same race occupies the entire territory from the Drave to the Lake of Scutari; and from the

hardly be stated here, though it will be seen later that nothing has been added to the Croats except opportunity.

Throughout the eighteenth century the policy of the Austrian Government was to repress as far as possible the Slavonic peoples that lay under its rule. Bohemia, which had lost its independence at the Thirty Years' War, was intellectually the "desert" which the Emperor Ferdinand had wished to make it; and the same drastic measures, though for somewhat different reasons, were applied to the subject races that fringed the southern border. Croatia in particular was used merely as an outpost against Turkish invasion: "purchased," as Dr. Kuhač says, "with a few empty political concessions," but kept in reality under the close discipline of a barrack-state. "We were not allowed,"

Roumanian frontier to the Adriatic. There is some Italian population in the extreme west, *e.g.*, at Zara; but most of this region is exclusively Slavonic, and the Servo-Croatian language prevails with certain modifications over the whole of it. There is also a considerable Croat population in Istria, Carniola, Lower Austria, and the adjoining parts of Hungary.

he continues, "to provide for our people the advantages of a real city, we had no centre of intellectual life and progress, and it was considered a sufficient privilege if the name of capital was bestowed upon one or other of our towns."*

Naturally, the Croatian nobles spent as little time as possible in their own country. It was much more amusing to stay at Pressburg or Vienna, where there were balls and theatres and pageants, and a man could see life. And so it happened that even the chance of patronage was denied, and the people sank to a state of apathy, their gifts forgotten, their voice starved into silence. But about 1835, the poet Ljudevit Gaj began, as Tyl was doing in Bohemia, to restore from its suspended animation the intellectual life of his countrymen. He settled their alphabet. He made their grammar. He collected the folksongs from every village and hamlet, and enriched them with lyrics of his own. He sowed dragon's teeth over the length and breadth

* Josip Haydn, p. 3.

of the country, and there sprang up as if by magic a crop of artists. Of course they were not of any great European importance. Lisinski and Franz von Suppé are the most famous among their musicians—but the whole lesson had to be learned anew, and these men were the first pupils.* And when the revolutions of 1848 gave fresh impulse to national life, a second chapter opened in the Croatian renascence, and, under the patronage of Bishop Strossmayer, there rose into being a new artistic generation.† Here, again, the musicians rather lag behind the poets and the men of letters; there was no conservatorium, there was no satisfactory method of training, and the young talent was generally too poor to embrace the opportunities which foreign lands afforded. But, if as yet the quality of the work is slight and trivial, something at least should be said about its extraordinary volume and facility. And it should be added that the leaders of the present generation—Zajc, Vilhar,

* See Appendix A.   † See Appendix B.

Faller, Dr. Kuhač himself—are all making large use of the national melodies as material.

Meantime, while the fortunes of Croatia were at their lowest, an event of earlier occurrence was producing important consequences. The Southern Slavs had always been a migratory people. As early as 595 they occupied the Tyrolean Pusterthal, where they have left their mark, not only in the character of the inhabitants but in a large number of local names*; later, under stress of Turkish invasion, they colonised Montenegro; and in the fifteenth or sixteenth century a body of Eastern Croats—Bosnen or Wasser-Kroaten, as the Germans called them — settled in the district of Central Austria which extends from Lake Balaton north-west to the Danube. The new home was eminently suited to the development of the race. It was rich and fertile, with vine-clad hills and broad

---

* See Appendix C. and compare Dr. Mitterrutzer's "Slavisches aus dem Oestlichen Pusterthal in Tirol," quoted by Dr. Kuhač, Josip Haydn, p. 12.

stretches of alluvial plain, it was well wooded and well watered, it extended to Pressburg, the second city in the empire, and contained at least one other town of considerable note ; it was within easy reach of the great intellectual and artistic movements. There is little wonder that this region soon came to be regarded as the focus of Croatian life, and that the wealth which sought it for entertainment attracted in due course the talent which sought it for livelihood.

The number of the original immigrants is unknown, but by the eighteenth century they unquestionably formed the larger part of the population. In 1780 Pressburg contained rather less than 28,000 inhabitants, of whom about half are noted in the official census as Croats or Slavonians ; while the smaller towns and villages in the neighbourhood were mainly occupied by the newcomers, and are still, despite German and Magyar influence, largely affected by Slavonic traditions. One curious and rather bewildering consequence is that almost every place in the region has possessed two names, one the German, used for official purposes; the other, Slavonic, for the benefit of the population. And when we add that east of the Leitha the Slavonic name is being ousted by the Hungarian, it will be seen that the unsophisticated traveller may now and again be at some difficulty to ascertain his route. An amusing instance fell under my own experience during the summer of 1897. Wishing to make pilgrimages to Eisenstadt, where Haydn was Kapellmeister, and to Željez, where Schubert taught music to Countess Esterházy, I took a ticket at Vienna for the first of these places, only to find, when my watch informed me of my destination, that Eisenstadt and Željez were the same place, and that the name upon the railway-station was Kis Martom.*

It is something more than a coincidence that among all districts of Austria this area of Croatian settlement has been the most

* For other instances of Slavonic occupation and nomenclature see Appendix D.

fruitful in great musicians. Veit Bach, the grandfather of John Sebastian, was born at Pressburg ; so was Chopin's great hero, Johann Nepomuk Hummel. The Haydns came from a neighbouring village, the proper name of which — Trstnik — was despairingly translated by the Germans into Rohrau. Joseph Weigl was a native of Eisenstadt, so was Ivan Fuchs, who succeeded Hummel as Prince Esterházy's Kapellmeister. Liszt was born at Rustnik, near Oedenburg, Joachim at Kitsee, Ludwig Strauss at Pressburg, Carl Goldmark at Keszthely. And round this constellation there gathers a whole nebula of lesser stars* names unfamiliar, it may be, to English readers, but in their own country accepted and recognised. Of course it is not claimed that all these artists are of Croatian blood. Some unquestionably are not ; but there is at least an *a priori* likelihood that some of them belonged to the race which was numerically dominant, especially as that race was Slavonic and therefore musical, and on this

* See Appendix E.

general point a word may perhaps be said before we proceed to particularise in the case of Haydn.

Now, apart from his, it should be noted that none of the names given above are distinctively Slavonic in character. For this fact a simple reason suffices. There had long been spreading through the world of music a practice, originated in Europe by scholars and divines, of taking a *nom de guerre* which should either represent the sound or translate the meaning of the family name. Erasmus, Melanchthon, Stephanus are familiar instances in the world of letters, and following these august models Grobstimm became Baryphonus; Schneider, Sartorius; Glareau, Loritius; and the like. Musicians for the most part seem to have avoided Latin and taken in its place whatever language lay ready to hand for display or convenience. Thus two famous Bohemians called themselves Dussek and Gyrowetz; Beethoven's father occasionally appeared as Bethoff; and the list may be extended even to such grotesques as Gionesi and Coperario. This device was specially necessary to the Croatian who was aiming at a career. We know with what diligence poor Abel, fresh from the German vowel sounds, endeavoured to adapt his name to the requirements of a British public.* The need of adaptation is still greater when the language is one which hardly any foreigner can hope to pronounce. Thus it was that the Croatian words tended to drop out altogether, and to be replaced by some rough German or Italian equivalent; and so complete was the transformation that we have to look twice before recognising Beethoven's first violin in Župančić, or finding in Trtić the composer of the "Trillo del diavolo."† In like manner the words "Bach" and "Hummel" may very possibly have been translations of Croatian names, names

* He called himself successively Abel, Ebel, Ibel, and Eibel. But his patrons always moved a stage in advance, even completing the circle by pronouncing the diphthong as it is pronounced in the word "eight."

† For a list of such adaptations see Appendix F.

which are known to have existed in Pressburg and which bear the same meaning; while the family of Liszt, also claimed by Dr. Kuhač,* may have been Slavonic in origin, though by the time of the great pianist the Magyar element had predominated for about a century. At any rate there can be no reasonable doubt as to the Slavonic origin of Tartini, Dragonetti, Giornovichi, Zingarelli, and many other of Haydn's contemporaries. There may have been in them some intermixture of race, but the parent stock was Croatian.

We cannot, then, assert that there is any antecedent improbability in assigning Haydn to the Croats. They are a musical people, they formed the chief population of the district where he was born, they have a fair claim to other great musicians of his time. It follows that we should discuss the biographical evidence, and see what is to be made out of the record of Haydn's family.

And here attention should be called to three points. First, that the name Hajden

* Josip Haydn, p. 16. See note to Appendix E.

or Hajdin (with its derivative Hajdenić, Hajdinović, &c.) is of common occurrence throughout Croatia, and, in days when spelling was roughly phonetic, may easily have appeared in Austrian official documents as Haiden or Hayden, forms by which its pronunciation is exactly represented. Now among all the variants assumed by the name of the composer's family,* these two are the most frequent and the most authoritative. His great-grandfather—the first member of the house who can be traced—appears in the Hainburg register as Caspar Haiden; his grandfather, once by obvious error called Thomas Hayrn, is usually Hayden elsewhere, the contemporary monuments at Rohrau give Mathias Haiden as the name of his father and Josephus Hayden as his own. He himself seems to have used the dissyllabic form up to January, 1762, when he signs for salary at Eisenstadt "Giuseppe Hayden"; in the February of the same year he changes to the

* Dr. Pohl gives fourteen variants, and even his list is not exhaustive. There are at least six in documents relating to the composer himself. See Appendix G.

isgnature "Joseph Haydn" which he afterwards habitually adopted. Even then the majority of documents relating to him are conservative enough to retain the earlier orthography, and the monument in Count Harrach's park, which bears the name Josephus Hayden, was erected as late as 1794. Indeed, there can be little doubt that Haiden or Hayden was the family name, shortened to suit the Viennese convention, as for the same reason Händel used to be shortened to Händl.* Secondly, the name, in one or other of its variants, is widely spread over the whole district from Wiener-Neustadt to Oedenburg. Dr. Pohl found it in some ten or a dozen villages, many of which are claimed by Dr. Kuhač as Croatian, and in the country towns like Hainburg or Eisenstadt it is of course more frequent still. There is no need to remind the reader that this is precisely the region occupied, since the sixteenth century, by the

* See the announcement of "Alexander's Feast" (Vienna, 1812) preserved in the Gesellschaft library. Carpani spells the name Hendl.

C

Slavonic immigrants. Thirdly, the home of the entire Haydn family is situated at the centre of the district in question. Caspar was born within sight of the Hainburg walls, Thomas lived and died as a burgher of that town, Mathias, after a brief period of travel, settled at Rohrau some ten miles away, and the most adventurous of his brothers wandered no further afield than Frankenmarkt or Ungarisch-Altenburg. It fits well enough with this home-keeping temper that Joseph Haydn should have spent more than threescore and ten years of his life inside a thirty mile radius from his native place.

On the father's side, then, Haydn would seem to belong to the Slavonic race among whom he lived and worked.* Again, his mother was a native of Rohrau, in her day a

---

* It is fair to state that some etymologists derive the name Haiden from the district "Auf der Haid" near Hainburg. But this is very unlikely. The district is a narrow stretch of moorland, and could not account for the prevalence of the name through the whole country-side, to say nothing of the frequent occurrence in Croatia proper.

distinctively Croatian village,* and her maiden name of Koller—a *vox nihili* in German—is plausibly regarded by Dr. Kuhač as a phonetic variant of the Croatian Kolar "wheelwright."† Everything that we know about his look and character favour the supposition of Slavonic descent. The lean ugly kindly face with high cheek-bones, long nose, and broad prominent under lip, the keen grey eyes softened by a twinkle of humour, the thin wiry figure, the strong nervous hands; all these and their analogues may be seen to-day in any village where Slavonic blood is still pure; and though of course they afford no argument in themselves, they add a touch of corroborative evidence which is worth noting. To the same cause may be traced that intense love of sport which has left his name as a proverb at

* Its second title, "Trstnik," is significant enough. And at the present day it contain a good many Croats, especially among the poorer inhabitants.

† In like manner Pilar has been Germanised into Piller, Solar into Soller, Kresar into Kresser, and so on. See a list of such changes in Kuhač's Josip Haydn, pp. 17, 18.

Eisenstadt*; and something, too, of the conviviality which made him say that his best evenings were those spent with his comrades at the "Engel." His talk, like his music, was full of that obvious fun which raises a laugh by a sudden touch of the unexpected; so are hundreds of Croatian ballads and aphorisms.† The humour is sometimes primitive, as when a Croat will tell you, "It is as true as that two and two make seven"; sometimes it reaches a more respectable level, as the gibe at the Bosnian Brethren, "who were ordered to abstain from something in Lent, and therefore took no water in their wine." But good, bad, or indifferent, it marks a distinctive type of peasant character; and in remembering that Haydn was a genius we need not forget that he was a peasant. The same holds good, too, of his religious feeling. It is not without significance that we may turn from one

* To je lovac i ribar kao Haydn; i.e., as good a shot and fisherman as Haydn.

† See instances quoted by Dr. Kuhač, Josip Haydn, pp. 27-29.

of his scores, with its "In Nomine Domini" at the beginning, and its "Laus Deo" at the end, to read in our newspaper that another Croatian village has risen in revolt upon the bare report of an ecclesiastical change. His temper, it may be, had grown more equable than that of his uneducated countrymen ; it had not lost anything of their loyalty.

The reasons which have led to this indication of detail may easily be misunderstood. It is not, of course, contended that any race has the monopoly of these characteristics, or that it differs ethically from its neighbours except by the very important fact of the proportion in which they are blended. But when it appears that the more we study Haydn, and the more we study the Slavonic character, the closer becomes the accord between them, when every feature of the one finds its parallel in the prevailing qualities of the other, then we may surely infer that to the antecedent probability some weight is added by this estimate of internal evidence. And probability will strengthen to certitude if we realise that Haydn's music is saturated with Croatian melody, that the resemblances are beyond question, beyond attribution of coincidence, beyond any explanation but that of natural growth. Some of his tunes are folksongs in their simplest form, some are folksongs altered and improved, the vast majority are original, but display the same general characteristics. He would stand wholly outside the practice of the great composers if he wrote, by habitual preference, in an idiom that was not his own.

His acquaintance with these folk-tunes must have begun from his earliest years. His father, we know, was a good musician who used, of an evening, to sit by the cottage door at Rohrau, singing to the children until they plucked up their courage and joined in. And when Frankh carried off the boy for his first experience of schooling, it was only to Hainburg, the earlier home of the family, where he may well have heard the same ballads breaking the quiet of the market-place, or echoing under the great arch of the Wiener Thor. Then, no doubt, came a change; the splendid apparition of George Reutter, the halo of Imperial patronage, the ten years in the choir at St. Stephen's, the sharp struggle for existence when the boy's voice broke, and he was turned into the streets of Vienna to shift for himself. It is in every way natural that his first composition should show little direct trace of national influence. He was in his student period; like all students he was dominated by the authority of his models, and for a time his chief ambition was to master the form of Emanuel Bach, and emulate the counterpoint of the Gradus ad Parnassum. But from the days when he began to speak in his own voice the Slavonic qualities unmistakably appear. There is the same general shape of melody, the same repetition of phrases, the same oddity of rhythm and metre, the same fineness and sensitiveness of feeling; and that not once or twice in a composition, but throughout its entire length. The common employment of folk-songs dates from the Symphony in D major 1762) to the Salomon Symphonies of 1795;

they find their way into everything—hymns, quartets, divertimenti; not, of course, because Haydn had any need to take them, but because he loved them too well to leave them out. It will be remembered that for thirty years, from 1761 to 1790, he worked as Prince Esterházy's Kapellmeister in the very centre of the Croatian colony. He must have heard these songs every day, he must have set his life to their lilt and cadence; they were the melodies of his own people, the echoes of his own thought. No one is surprised that Burns should have gathered the Ayrshire peasant songs and transmuted them into gold by the fire of his genius; it is not more wonderful that Haydn should have enriched the treasures of Eisenstadt with metal from his native mines, and as Heine pertinently puts it, the Temple is built by the Architect, not by the stonecutters who supply him with his materials.

Among the numerous illustrations collected by Dr. Kuhač, the following deserve special attention.

A CROATIAN COMPOSER.

(1) The Cassation in G major (1765)* begins as follows :—

a melody noticeable for the breaking of the four-quaver rhythm by alternate bars of six. It can hardly be doubted that when Haydn wrote this he had in his mind the old Slavonic drinking song, " Nikaj na svetu "—

variants of which may still be heard in Croatia, and in the Carinthian Zillerthal. Similar instances of slight adaptation may be traced from the spring song, "Proljeće"—

* Dr. Kuhač gives 1754 as the date of this work. If so, it is the earliest known instance. The above date, which is more probably correct, is that given by Dr. Pohl.

which appears at the beginning of the D major Quartet (Op. 17, No. 6) as—

and from the dance-song "Hajde malo dere"—

which is thus altered by Haydn—

(2) The curious and characteristic finale of the D major Symphony (Salomon, No. 7) is founded on the following theme :—

This is simply an amended version of the popular ballad, "Oj Jelena," which belongs to the district of Kolnov, near Oedenburg, and is specially noted by Dr. Kuhač as being commonly sung in Eisenstadt. Its tune, essentially Slavonic in rhythm and cadence, runs thus:—

Variants of this melody are found in Croatia proper, Servia, and Carniola.*

It is probable that the other movements of this symphony are equally influenced by folksongs; in any case, no doubt can exist as to the Symphony in E♭, "Mit dem Paukenwirbel." The opening theme of the Allegro—

* See Kuhač, "South Slavonic Popular Songs," vol. iii. pp. 98-100.

is noted by Dr. Kuhač as Croatian.* The Andante is founded on two themes, the first minor—

the second major—

* See Kuhač, "South Slavonic Popular Songs," vol. iii. p. 92.

both of which are taken, and considerably improved, from two folksongs of the Oedenburg district, (*a*) "Na Travniku"—

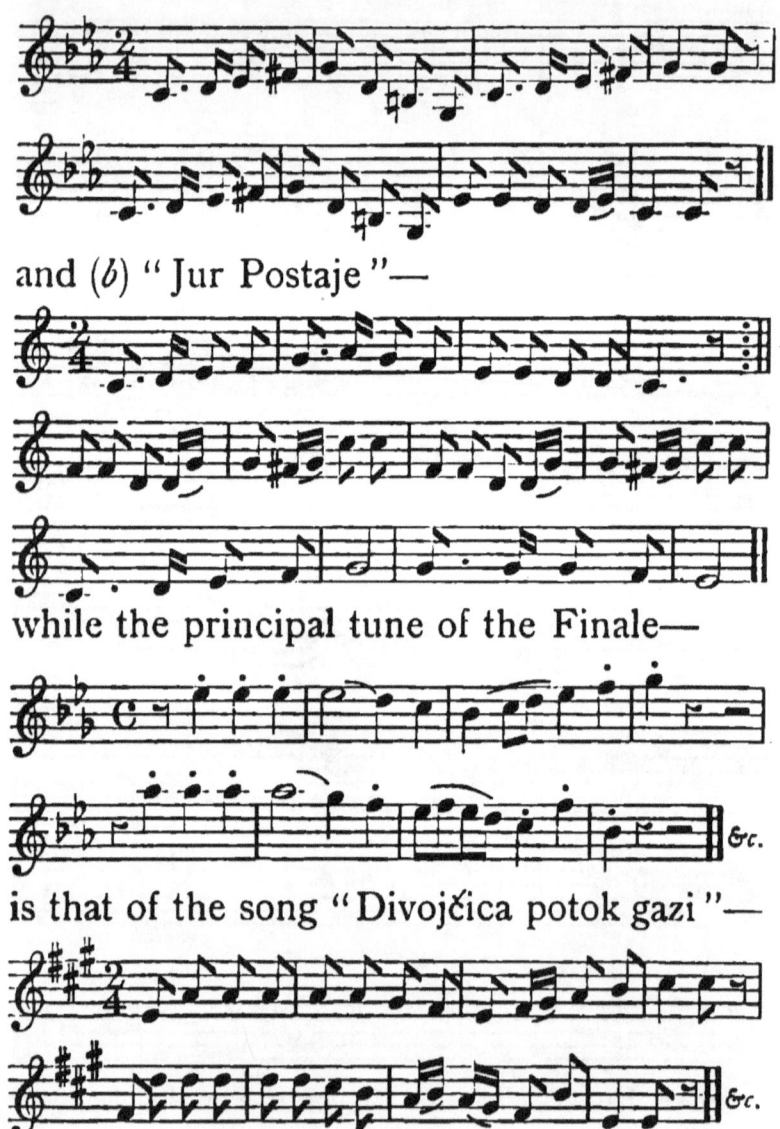

and (*b*) "Jur Postaje"—

while the principal tune of the Finale—

is that of the song "Divojčica potok gazi"—

which is common among the Croats, especially those of Haydn's district.* Again, the Trio of the A major Symphony (No. 11 in Haydn's Catalogue) contains a Slavonic melody—

and the first movement of its successor (D major, No. 12) suggests another—

(3) There are several cases in which, without direct adaptation, Haydn has shown the same tendency of thought or phrase as the Slavonic folksongs. A favourite "curve" of his may be illustrated by the opening of the B♭ Symphony (Salomon, No. 9)—

as well as by the Dalmatian Overture of

* See Kuhač, "South-Slavonic Popular Songs," vol. iii. p. 82.

Franz von Suppé and the tunes (from Zara and Borištov) on which it was founded—*e.g.*, the ballad " Na placi sem stal "—

Another, even more beautiful, ends the opening strain in the Adagio of the G major Quartet (Op. 77, No. 1)—

and appears also in the Croatian " Čuješ doro dobro moje "—

while the use of the unprepared dominant ninth, constructed out of a dominant seventh by shifting the melody a third higher, was not so common in Haydn's day that we can afford to neglect the resemblance of—

A CROATIAN COMPOSER. 49

quoted by Dr. Kuhač from a Quartet in B ♭,* to—

from a popular folksong of Carniola.

(4) These latter examples do not imply reminiscences, but at most a general sympathy of temper. A good deal more, however, is involved in the treatment of Slavonic dance tunes. It is hardly too much to say that what the Csardas was to Liszt the Kolo was to Haydn; with this difference—that the earlier and greater musician has throughout made a finer use of his materials. The Kolo is a Slavonic measure, which I have seen the children dance at Agram and the men at Sarajevo,

* Dr. Kuhač calls it the Sixth Quartet ("u Allegru šestoga četverogudja"), but it is not the sixth in the Paris and London edition, or in the Dresden, or in that of Peters.

bright and cheery of movement, its tune in two-four time ingeniously varied by patterns of quaver and semiquaver figures. Here, for instance, is an example well known in Bosnia and Dalmatia :—

and used with an amended cadence in the Finale of the C major Quartet (Op. 33, No. 3) :—

Here, again, is a similar dance-tune from Servia, which opens the Symphony in D major (Haydn's Catalogue, No. 4) :—

and here another in the Finale of the G major Quartet (Op. 77, No. 1) :—

in which so wonderful an effect is produced by the alternation of cold unison and glowing harmonies.

Many of Haydn's characteristic melodies follow one or other of these types: *e.g.*, this from the Finale of the F major Quartet (Op. 74, No. 2)—

or this from the "Bear" Symphony:—

or this from the Finale of the Quartet in D (Op. 76, No. 5):—

while the metrical peculiarities of the Eastern or Servian Slav may be illustrated by the following, from the Symphony in F major (No. 1 in the Viennese edition) :—

as they may, apart from the Kolo measure, in a hundred of his minuets and finales. Again, the early Pianoforte Concerto in D major ends with an oddly named "Rondo à l'Hongrie, the principal subject of which is as follows :—

This melody, which contains no Magyar characteristics, either of figure, scale, or stanza, is compressed from that of the Siri Kolo, as commonly danced in Bosnia and Dalmatia. The complete tune runs :—

a typical rustic dance, which in Haydn's hands has gained not only by compression, but by a more artistic accompaniment.

(5) In addition to the dance measure, Haydn has adopted other instrumental forms, *e.g.*, marches, bag-pipe melodies, and the like. Here is one, with a strange rhythm, from the Pianoforte Scherzando in F major :—

and here, from the Finale of the B♭ Symphony (Salomon, No. 9), is the march which is commonly played in Turopol at rustic weddings :—

Another Croatian march beginning—

has been identified by Dr. Kuhač from an unpublished Symphony in A major, and there is a further example from the Allegro of the B♭ Quartet (Op. 71, No. 1)—

(6) The two most remarkable instances are yet to come. According to a well-known story, Prince Esterházy once discussed with his Kapellmeister the question whether Church music could not be made " at the same time religious and popular." It is hard to realise that Haydn's Masses were ever regarded as too severe ; in any case, the Prince felt dissatisfied, and wanted a change. He had recently returned from his annual pilgrimage to Maria Zell. He had heard there music which pleased him, and he seems to have suggested that in the Eisenstadt chapel there was too much counterpoint and too little melody. Haydn listened, sent to Maria Zell for information, bided his time, and, when next year the day of the pilgrimage was approaching, wrote a " Mass " or Service to German words,* despatched it to the famous church, had it

* This story is sometimes told of the Mariazeller Mass in C major (Novello, No. 15). But first, the Mariazeller Mass was written by commission for Anton Liebe von Kreutzner ; second, it is set to the usual Latin text ; and third, it does not contain any of the popular melodies in question.

secretly practised, and finally found an excuse for slipping off on a holiday. The Prince came back more dissatisfied than ever. "I have heard," he said, "a service of Church music composed and played in a style which you will never equal." "Your Highness," answered Haydn, "the composition was mine, and I was the organist."

From this "Mass," of which at present no other trace seems to be discoverable, Dr. Kuhač quotes seven melodies on the authority of the Dominican Alois Russwurm, who was a personal friend of Haydn, and by whom the story was originally recorded.

The first, "Hier liegt vor Deiner Majestät," is the opening theme of the first number—

and comes from the Croatian tune—

The second, "Gott soll gepriesen werden"—

is the song "Ti jabuka," as sung in Velik-Borištov—

The third, "Allmächtiger, vor Dir im Staube,"—

begins remarkably like the Slavonian drinking song, "Draga moja gospodo."*

* The three-bar phrase is a common feature of early Slavonic melodies, especially when conjoined with a second phrase of four bars in irregular balance.

The fourth, "O Vater, sieh vor Deinem Throne"—

may fairly be regarded as a variant of the Dalmatian song, "Jedna Ciganka"—

The fifth, "Betrachtet ihn in Schmerzen"—

is almost identical in both parts with the following Croatian melody:—

The sixth — "Nun ist das Lamm geschlachtet"—

is derived partly from two separate strains in the Croatian and Slavonian versions of a convivial chorus—"Vivla compagnija"—

(a)—

(b)—

partly from a Croatian sacred song—"Stani gori gospodar."

The seventh — "Dich wahres Oesterlamm"—which is the concluding phrase of the canticle for the Celebration,—

borrows its exact sequence and its curious halting rhythm from the Croatian "Miši prave svatove"—

A CROATIAN COMPOSER.   63

Clearly, in Haydn's vocabulary "popular" meant Slavonic.

It may be objected that this example proves nothing. Grant that Haydn was living in a certain district, and that he was asked for once to write in a popular style; what more natural than that he should adapt himself to his surroundings, and use the idioms that he found in common currency? A man readily drops into dialect when he is addressing a rural audience, and does not become a countryman by seasoning his discourse with a few country proverbs and metaphors. This rejoinder would be of more effect if the "Mass" were an isolated phenomenon: it somewhat loses weight when we remember that the music only turns to Church use the tendencies that have already been noted in symphony and quartet. Still, our case would undoubtedly be stronger if we could find Haydn appealing, in the same tongue, to the Austrian Empire at large, and using the native Slavonic for some great political or ceremonial occasion. Here, at any rate, is a test which we may reasonably regard as crucial, and which, if successfully applied, should go some way towards settling the question.

Unfortunately, the Croatian melodies are not, as a rule, well suited for such a purpose. They are bright, sensitive, piquant, but they seldom rise to any high level of dignity or earnestness. They belong to a temper which is marked rather by feeling and imagination than by any sustained breadth of thought, and hence, while they enrich their own field of art with great beauty, there are certain frontiers which they rarely cross, and from which, if once crossed, they soon return. One limitation in particular will have been observed by every student. It frequently happens that a Croatian or Servian tune will begin with a fine phrase, and then fall to an anticlimax—either losing sight of its tonality, or wavering in its rhythm, or ending with a weak or commonplace cadence. In almost all the examples quoted above, it is the opening of the tune which Haydn has borrowed; its conclusion he has nearly always improved or re-written.* And the reasons that impelled him to this practice may be illustrated by the following variants, in all of which are apparent the same touch of inspiration, and the same weakness of development.

(*a*) The song "Stal se jesem," as sung in Marija Bistrict—

* See in particular the song "Na travniku" (p. 46), and the first Kolo tune (p. 50).

† The musical stanza, in this song, goes to a half-stanza of the words. The first is—

Stal se jesem rano jutro   *i.e.*, In the early morning stood I
  Malo pred zorjum.   Close upon the dawn.

(*b*) The same song as it appears in the district of S. Ivan Zeline—

(*c*) The same as it appears at Medjumur (Murinsel)—

In these versions the last four bars appear to have been loosely attached to the rest of tune; at any rate, they are often found, apart from the first phrase, in Croatian carols and drinking songs. Again, among other districts there has been some rearrangement of the words, with corresponding changes in the music. Either the opening line is not repeated, which leads to the excision of the third bar, and a consequent alteration of cadence; *e.g.*—

(*d*) Variant from Kolnov (near Oedenburg)—

or it is inserted again after the second, so as to give the stanza an alternation of masculine and feminine endings; *e.g.*—

(*e*) Variant from Čembe—

The rest is easily divined. When in 1797 Haydn was commissioned to set the National Anthem, he must have had this tune before his eye, and have determined to use it as the pedestal of the *monumentum ære perennius* which his loyalty erected.*
And here a word may be said as to the manner in which the great tune appears to have been written. It was no momentary inspiration, no sudden impromptu that should come into existence at full growth; like most of Beethoven's music, it was made carefully, and by deliberate weighing of alternatives. By a piece of singular good fortune, we are for once admitted to the master's workshop, and allowed to take our lesson in melody by the observation of his practice.

Now the second strain of the folk-tune is too short to fit the second line of the poem;

---

* There is no need to discuss here the question of Telemann's Rondo. If its resemblance to Haydn's tune be anything more than fortuitous, it is probably referable to the same source. See Josip Haydn, p. 81.

accordingly, Haydn began by extending its cadence, and instead of—

wrote—

following it with repeat-marks, after the common method of primary form. Two other changes explain themselves. The measure is dignified by the broader time-signature, and the accent shifted from arsis to thesis by the rearrangement of the bars. Otherwise, in the first half of the stanza the folk-tune remains unaltered.

But for the second half it was manifestly insufficient. Both the possible variants are too trivial, and one too brief, to afford the requisite climax. As a natural consequence, Haydn discarded both, and proceeded to supply their place with two original strains, which in the Autograph sketch* run as

* Preserved in the Museum of the Gesellschaft Library at Vienna. It is a small oblong sheet, similar to those on which Haydn wrote his "Canons," and contains, first, the complete sketch of the melody—

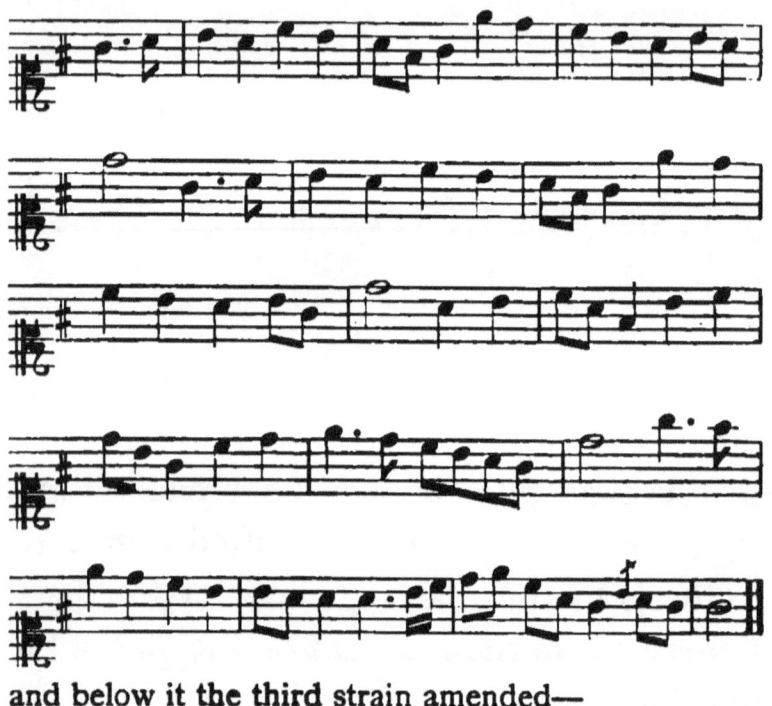

and below it the third strain amended—

The improved version of the fourth strain is not there, but, curiously enough, Pohl notes an anticipation of it in the Mariazeller Mass. See Pohl's Haydn, vol. ii. p. 333.

follows :—

Still, he was dissatisfied with the result, and it is easy to suggest the reason. In the former of these two strains there is a passage which carries tonic harmony—out of place at this stage of the tune—and its cadence, moreover, rhymes awkwardly with that of the half-stanza. The latter of the two comes down from its point of stress with a fine sweeping movement, but, three bars from the end, breaks its melodic curve into two distinct pieces, and so loses continuity of line. Both were accordingly corrected, one on the same page, the bottom stave of which bears, in hasty manuscript, the amended form—

the other, with a few more minute alterations, at a later period of the work. And thus, of such diverse metal as Cellini cast his "Perseus," did Haydn beat out the melody by which he has given voice to a nation's patriotism.

It is to be hoped that these examples will not encourage any reader to pursue Haydn with the cry of plagiarist. No accusation could be more unfounded or more unreasonable. He poached upon no man's preserve, he robbed no brother-artist, he simply ennobled those peasant-tunes with the thought and expression of which he was most nearly in accord. The whole extent of his indebtedness is at most an occasional melody, and is often but a single phrase; the treatment, the setting, the workmanship belong as truly to him as Faust to Goethe, or Cymbeline to Shakespeare. The master who has written a hundred and twenty first-rate symphonies, and eighty-three first-rate quartets, may surely claim the right to take his wealth where he finds it; and if we are churlish enough to deny this, at least we may allow him the privilege of speaking in his native tongue. To Haydn, the folk-tunes were little more than the words of his accustomed speech, hardly obscured when the Church asserted her contrapuntal dignity, and reappearing in full significance when he returned to the untrammelled orchestra and the freedom of the four magic strings. It is more important to note how closely his special melodic gift is in sympathy with that of his people. Many of the tunes quoted above are among those which a critic would select as especially characteristic: there are literally hundreds of his invention by which, in a more or less degree, the same qualities are exhibited. No doubt he was not only the child of his nation, he had his own personality, his own imaginative force, his own message to deliver in the ears of the world. But through all these the national element runs as a determining thread. That "les grands artistes n'ont pas de patrie" is a sentence abundantly refuted by its very author; it assuredly finds no support in the life of the Croatian peasant who has made immortal the melodies of his race.

A new aspect of the question has been brought into prominence by recent history. The course of policy pursued in our own day by the Austrian Government is tending to reverse the relative importance of the Croatian colony and of the mother-country from which it sprang. On the one hand, the central provinces are being steadily Germanised, the Slavonic language is beginning to die out, the Slavonic blood to be crossed by intermixture, and though yet the change is only in process, there is no lack of indication that it is operative. Along the western bank of the Leitha, German is now the prevailing speech, along the eastern bank it is disputing the palm with Hungarian, and between them the Slav, for all his tenacity, will some day be dislodged or absorbed. Hardly any inhabitant speaks of Požun now; the name is either Pozsony or Pressburg; Liesing has almost forgotten that it was once Lesnik, and though Oedenburg* still remains as a fortress, it is becoming more and more isolated as the years advance. But, on the other hand, a wider range of opportunity is being opened in Croatia proper. The impulse towards national life, started as we have already seen by Ljudevit Gaj, is being wisely fostered and encouraged by Imperial patronage; and Agram, which a century ago was a little country town, is now assuming the state and dignity of a capital. The University, founded in 1874, has already done much for the study of art and letters; the old market-place has become a fine square, with an opera-house in the centre; the waste ground to the south has been laid out in public gardens, and enclosed with galleries and museums. It is natural that the present race should follow these changes

* Its Croatian name, "Sopron," is still in current use, and it contains enough Slavonic inhabitants to employ their language in many of its official notices.

with keen enthusiasm; and should look forward eagerly and confidently to the days of coming greatness. Nor even to a stranger are the evidences lacking. The tone may be somewhat Chauvinist, the self-gratulation somewhat indiscriminate, the record of present achievement a little wanting in distinction; but as yet the movement is new, the resources are new, the whole field has to be contested step by step. It would be idle to expect another Haydn at present; the line has been broken, and must rally before it can advance. Enough for the moment that there are force and impetus and courage, that there is active and restless ability, that there is an unswerving determination to win the day. Who knows in what recruit's knapsack the bâton of the field-marshal may be lying hidden?

For in all the music of this century there is no phenomenon more remarkable than the steady progress of the Slavonic race. As early as 1818 an English critic was far-sighted enough to predict the advent of

Russia,* and though his readers never lived to see the presage fulfilled, though in his generation there appeared no greater name than that of Glinka, yet our own day has verified his words beyond the possibility of cavil. There may be some difference of opinion about Rubinstein, there can be none about Borodin or Tschaikowsky, and the traditions which they set are being ably followed by a whole school of younger composers. Toward the middle of the century came Chopin,

* The passage is worth quoting entire for more than one reason. "Nor can we imagine the art is on the decline while so great a genius as Beethoven lives. This author, though less perfect in other respects than Haydn, exceeds him in power of imagination; and from recent specimens of his unbounded fancy it is to be expected that he will extend the art in a way never contemplated even by Haydn or Mozart. If we were inclined to push our speculations further upon this point we might refer to the very extraordinary discoveries that are now making in Russia in the department of instrumental music. In the course of twenty years it is probable that such effects will be produced in that country as will lead to the most important results in the science of sounds."
—W. Gardiner, in the translation of Stendhal's "Letters on Haydn," 2nd edition (London, 1818), page 3.

whose chief ambition, as he himself said, was "to be the Uhland of his country," and whose chief work was to stamp with the impress of a classic his national strains of polonaise and mazurka. Some thirty years ago Smetana's brilliant comedy laid the foundation on which Dvořák has built, and rescued from disuse and oblivion the folk-songs of Bohemia. It is not without interest that we see another Slavonic nation re-entering the field. In one sense it was the leader of them all, in another it is the latest accession to their ranks, and its fortunes, as it tries to regain a lost position, should be watched by us not only with encouragement, but with close and intimate sympathy.

For, *de nobis fabula narratur.* Western Europe also knows of a land which was once a leader in musical art, which forewent its trust, which suffered its voice to be silenced, which allowed its musicians to bid for popularity by adopting foreign names and foreign methods, which is now striving, with better opportunities than any Slavonic nation can possess, to recover the old ground, and recall the forgotten message. If we disdain the comparison we may learn humility by reading the estimate in which we have long been held by our neighbours. " English music," says a recent German historian, " may be said to end with Purcell " ; " English art," say our French critics, " has long degenerated into imitation " ; and though our present leaders are nobly refuting the charge, there is still with us too much of that cosmopolitan temper which is among the most insidious of our enemies. No doubt times are improving. In Leeds, in Birmingham, in Bristol, even in London, the Englishman may get a hearing, though unless he write Royalty ballads he will hardly find a publisher. But his audience is not yet attuned into proper sympathy with his work. We still judge too much by reference to alien ideals, we are still too indifferent to our own natural language, and our own natural cast of thought. And, until we shake off this indifference and learn to extend our patriotism to our art, we shall never resume our place as a great musical nation.

There is no need that we should offer a less cordial welcome to our foreign visitors, or a less cordial recognition of the immense service that they have done. "Was macht dieser Fremde hier?" is not patriotism, but discourtesy, a mark of the weakness which fears to meet the world frankly upon equal terms. At the same time we have no right either to neglect or to depreciate our own. A great artistic school is not built in a single moment or in a single generation; the work is long, heavy, difficult; it is easily discouraged, it is easily retarded, it needs all the care and diligence that it can command. And there is one way, and one only, in which we can bring it to a successful issue. Let us cut our timber from our own forests, let us quarry our stone from the bed-rock of our own nation, and then let our master-builders deal with the matter as their genius shall determine.

A most hopeful sign is the revival of interest in our national melodies. To the artists who have collected them, to the artists who are making them familiar, our cordial gratitude is due. But it is not enough to have them, we must use them; and it is not enough to use them, we must learn how to catch their spirit. Haydn had a far slighter material than ours, yet he could use it to a purpose which will be remembered when all our exotic romances are forgotten. And now that more than one English master is showing us the way, we have no excuse, we have no pretext for withholding our allegiance any longer.

It is now some years since a few English writers began to advocate the return to nationalism. Since then, much, no doubt, has been done, but much still remains to do, and to us hearers a great part of the reform is entrusted. We have listened to foreign tongues until our own sounds odd and unfamiliar. We have sat so long at Trimalchio's banquet that we have no appetite left for our native fare. Extremes of passion, extremes of languor, inordinate appeals to sense, all these are alien from our national temper, and we are growing surfeited with them until our taste is spoiled and our palate vitiated. It is just the same in the world of letters. "No one reads Scott," says one critic; "No one wants Shakespeare," says another; "give us d'Annunzio and Sudermann and the Immoral Philosophy of Friedrich Nietzsche." Fortunately English ethics and English literature may be left to look after themselves; they have both a continuity of tradition which will prevent them from falling very far askew. But our art of music is being restored from the heaps of ruin into which it was laid two centuries ago, and it is the business of all who care for art or country to lend a hand. At least we might try to discover what English music has to say, and estimate our composers according to their capacity for saying it.

This position is strengthened by all evidence of musical history. The same hand which made Germany a people enriched her with the "Marseillaise of the Reformation," and so founded the long dynasty of her great composers. Art in

France was at its lowest, when the chief occupation of Paris was to dispute between the claims of the Bavarian Gluck and the Italian Piccinni. Italy herself declined as she lost her national character, the Slavonic peoples have advanced as they have reasserted theirs. And what is true of nations is equally true of their leaders. "The greatest genius," says Emerson, "is the most indebted man"; the man, that is, who can turn to the most noble and enduring use the traditions of his age and country. So it was with Haydn. Nothing can be more false than to regard him as merely a Court musician, writing with ready and facile talent the *pièces d'occasion* that were needed for the theatre or the reception-room. His life at Eisenstadt gave him opportunity such as no composer had ever before enjoyed, but the patronage was too enlightened and the character too strong to be satisfied with work that was mannered or artificial. Under the famous "livery of blue and silver" there beat the heart of a rustic poet, full of kindliness, of drollery, of good-fellowship, of the love of children and animals. His genius, trained by years of assiduous labour, gave him a complete mastery over the inherited resources of his art, his imagination extended them with fresh discoveries and inventions. But throughout the whole his favourite themes are pastoral, songs of the shepherd and the harvester, songs of country courtship, songs of the vintage feast and the jovial holiday. It is little wonder that he should speak in the language of his people, or recall the phrases that had been familiar from his childhood.

Yet it is no patois that he uses, but the speech of a whole nation; a living force that spreads wide and reaches to distant boundaries. Nor is he great because he has chosen this or that topic, this or that form of utterance; it is because he is great that there was no choice in the matter. He could not have written of set habit in the German idiom; he was Slav by race and Slav by temper, and his music is too genuine to present itself in foreign guise. It is from this point of view that we should understand him; not by loosely classifying him among a people with whom he had little in common, but by regarding him as the true embodiment of his own national spirit. The Greek proverb condemns a man of two tongues : through the world of art the condemnation is still in force, and at least some measure of it should fall on the ingenious critics who call patriotism parochial, and justify their epithet by obliterating frontiers.

APPENDICES.

APPENDIX A.

Croatian Musicians, 1835-1848.

(1) *Composers* :—Lisinski.   Čačković.
                 Livadić.   Štoos.
                 Wiesner.   Mašek.
                 Rusan.   Baron Prandau.
                 Pintavić.   F. von Suppé.
                 Jaić.

(2) *Singers* :— Countess Rubido. Stazić.
                 Štriga.   Ledenig.

(3) *Virtuosi, &c.* :—
                 Ivan Padovec.   L. A. Zellner.

N.B.—The following rules of pronunciation should be observed.

r (as a semi-vowel) carries a very short vowel sound before the consonant. Brlog = Berlog made as near a monosyllable as possible.

c = tz. Zajc is pronounced Zaitz.

č = ch soft (like ch in Church).

ć = ty in which the y is a consonant (as it is for instance in the word "you"). The sound is half-way between the "te" in "righteous" and the "tch" in "wretched."

š = sch or sh. Pušovec (see Appendix C) is pronounced Pushovetz.

ž = the French j, as in jour.

lj and nj are like the gli and gn in figlio, campagna.

The other letters are, roughly speaking, pronounced as in German, except z, which = s in sehr; and s, which = ss in Strasse.

APPENDIX B.

Croatian Musicians, 1848-1880.

(1) *Composers :—*

Rihar.*	G. Eisenhut.
Vilhar.*	A. Mihalović.
Fleišman.*	Kociančić*
Köck.	Leban.*
Epstein.	Valenta.*
Zajc.	Slava Atanasijevic.
Strmic.	Faller.
Just.	Kuhač.

(2) *Singers :—*

Ema Murska.	Grbić.
Matilda Marlov.	Kašman.
Matilda Mallinger.	Nolli.*
Ema Vizjak.	Maria Kotas.
Irma Terputec.	Maria Pikril.
Mazoleni.	Maca Matačić

Sofia Kramberger.

* Slovenian.

APPENDICES. 89

(3) *Virtuosi* :—
    Šteiner.   Petrié.
    Hummel.   Ivan Mihalović.
    Ludmilla Veizer.   F. Krežma.
    Josif Eisenhut.   Anka Krežma.
    Ciol.   Kolander.

(4) *Conductors, Professors, &c.* :—
    Kukulević.   Antun Švarc.*
    B. Ipavec.   Martin Jenko.
    G. Ipavec.   Adolf Schwartz.
            Ida Wimberger.

APPENDIX C.

Croatian Names in the Pusterthal and Neighbourhood

Germanised form :—	*Croatian form* :—
Aegrathal.	Ograda.
Arvig (?).	Oranik.
Berlogaz.	Brlog.
Bschwoitz.	Pušovec.
Dolnitz.	Dolina.
Frutscherthal.	Vručidol.
Garnitza.	Krnica.
Glanz	Klanjec.
Glinz (Linz).	Glinica.
Gollisel.	Goloselo.

    * Possibly German, see " Schwartz " below.

Germanised form :—	Croatian form :—
Gruschgize.	Kruškica.
Kollnig.	Kolnik.
Kräll.	Kralj.
Libisel.	Ljubisel.
Lasser.	Lesar.
Lessing.	Lešnik.
Motschenboden.	Mocva.
Pedoll.	Podolje.
Petsch.	Peč (Pešti).
Plötsch.	Ploca.
Polliz.	Polica.
Pusterthal	Pustodol.
Rudenek.	Rudnik.
Stoanitzbrunn.	Studenac.
Stollizen.	Stolica.
Tragen.	Draga.
Tristach.	Trstje.
Villgraten.	Velegrad.
Zabemig.	Zavrhnik.
Zelzach.	Selca.
Zuchepoll.	Suhopolje.

NOTE.—For similar examples in other parts of Austria, see Kämmel's "Die Anfänge deutschen Lebens in Oesterreich."

APPENDIX D.

Traces of Croat Population in the District near Pressburg.

The following towns and villages have possessed a

APPENDICES. 91

Croat population, either predominant or at least considerable :—

Maiersdorf.	Wildungsmauer.
Zverndorf.	Kaglor.
Pangort.	Pišelsdorf.
Marchegg.	Mannersdorf.
Bratisey.	Au (Cindrov).
Senfeld.	Hof (Cimov).
Hlohovac.	Landeck.
Siebenbrunn.	Kroatisch Wagram
Horisey.	(Ogran hrvatski).
Štrandorf.	Frama,
Poturno.	Fuchspichl
Limisdorf.	(Fukšpil).
Andlersdorf	Ort.
(Razvitnjak).	Bratštatin.
Guštatin.	Lower Siebenbrunn.
Petronel.	Kroatisch Haslern
Rohrau (Trstnik).	(Hazlor hrvatski).

Besides the whole district round Eisenstadt, Oedenburg, and the Neusiedler See.

APPENDIX E.

Musicians born in Pressburg and its Neighbourhood.

* * Hans Neusiedler, Lutenist, born 1563 near the Neusiedler See.
* * Veit Bach, grandfather of J. S. Bach, born about 1580 at Pressburg.

* Probably Croatian.

- * Andreas Rauch, organist and composer, born about 1590 at Pottendorf.
- * Samuel Bockshorn (Capricornus), conductor, born in 1629 at Pressburg.
- * J. S. Kusser (Couser), composer, born in 1657 at Pressburg.
- * Joseph Haydn, born in 1732 at Rohrau.
- * Michael Haydn, born in 1737 at Rohrau.
- * Johann Evangelist Haydn, born in 1743 at Rohrau.
- * Matthias Kamiensky (Kamenar), composer, born in 1734 at Oedenburg.
- Theodor Lotz, musical instrument maker, born about 1740 at Pressburg.
- * Anton Zimmermann, composer, born in 1741 at Pressburg.
- * N. Hadrava, Lutenist, born in 1750 near Pressburg.
- * G. Druschetzky (Druzechi), composer, born about 1760 at Pressburg. (?)
- Jacob Hyrtl, oboe-player in the Esterházy orchestra, born about 1760 at Eisenstadt.
- Joseph Weigel (Weigl), composer, born in 1766 at Eisenstadt.
- * Ivan Bihari, violinist and composer, born in 1769 at Great Abony.
- * Stephan Koch, musical instrument maker, born in 1772 at Vesprim.
- * Ivan Fuss, composer, born in 1777 at Tolnau.
- * Johann Nepomuk Hummel, born in 1778 at Pressburg.

* Probably Croatian.

APPENDICES.

* Joseph Blahak, composer, born in 1779 at Raggersdorf.
* Ivan Fuchs, Kapellmeister to Prince Esterházy, born in 1780 at Eisenstadt.
  Peter Lichtenthal, composer, born in 1780 at Pressburg.
  Count Thadeus Amadé, pianist, born in 1783 at Pressburg.
* Adolf Müller, composer, born in 1802 at Tolnau.
* Joseph Wurda, singer, born in 1807 at Gjur (Raab).
* Friedrich Fischer, singer, born in 1809 at Pressburg.
† Franz Liszt, born in 1811 at Raiding (Rudnik).
  Michael Hauser, violinist, born in 1822 at Pressburg.
* Ferdinand Kletzer, violoncellist, born in 1830 at Oedenburg. (?)
  Joseph Joachim, born in 1831 at Kitsee.
  Carl Goldmark, born in 1832 at Keszthelyn.
  Ludwig Straus, born in 1845 at Pressburg.
  Leopold Auer, violinist, born in 1845 at Vesprim.
  Charlotte Debner, violinist, born in 1846 at Kitsee.

* Probably Croatian.

† The case of Liszt is somewhat apart from the others. The earliest form of his name appears to be Listhius, which Dr. Kuhač claims with some plausibility as Slavonic (naše gore list). But as early as 1747 the Magyarised form appears in the person of Canon Johann Liszt; and there can be little doubt that by the time of the great pianist's birth the family had become thoroughly Hungarian. There are, of course, many Hungarian families in which Magyar and Slavonic strains are united, and in the music of Liszt the Magyar element unquestionably predominates.

APPENDIX F.

Names of Croatian Musicians Translated or Corrupted.

(a) *Translated* (equivalent of meaning : conjectural).

Current Name.	Croatian Name.
Neusiedler.	Novosel.
Bockshorn.	Rožić.
Bach.	Potočić or Potočniak.
Rauch.	Dimić or Dimović.
Zimmermann.	Tesar, or Tesarević.
Koch.	Kuhač, Kuhačević, or Kuharević.
Fuss.	Nogić, or Nogavac.
Hummel.	Bumbarević or Ćmeliak.*
Fuchs.	Lissa, Lisica, or Lisinski.
Müller.	Mlinar or Mlinarić.
Fischer.	Ribar or Ribarić.

(b) *Corrupted* (adaptation of sound : reasonably certain).

Bulgarelli.	Bugarin.
Bona.	Bunić.
Brusa.	Brusić.
Draghi.	Dragi.
Dragonetti.	Draganić.
Ferrich.	Ferić.
Gerlo..	Grlo.

* According to the two meanings of the word Hummel.

APPENDICES. 95

Giornovichi.	Jarnović.
Jelich or Jael.	Jelić.
Kresnik.	Gresnik.
Henkel.	Kengelović.
Calinde.	Kalin.
Kannabich.	Kanabić.
Cola.	Kola.
Muzin.	Mužina.
Mazoleni.	Mazolić.
Mazzuranna.	Mašuranić.
Nachich or Nanchini.	Nakić.
Pollini.	Polić.
Desplanes.	Polinar.
Pisaroni.	Pisar.
Zappa.	Sapa.
Scalichius.	Skalić.
Smetenich.	Smetenić.
Tamparizza.	Tamparica.
Thern.	Trn.
Tartini.	Trtić.
Tuscan.	Tuskan
Visochi.	Visoki.
Zingarelli.	Ciganin.
Zagitz.	Zaic.
Zuchetto.	Zuketić.
Schuppanzigh.	Županćić.

APPENDIX G.

Variants of the Name "Haydn" within the Limits of the Composer's Family.

(a) *Haiden :* Register of Caspar Haiden's marriage, Hainburg, 1657.
Register of Joseph Haiden's death, Hainburg, April 19, 1715.
Register of the composer's baptism, Rohrau, April 1, 1732 (the father's name is given as Mathias Haiden).
Register of his mother's death, Rohrau, February 25, 1754.

(b) *Hayden :* Register of Thomas Hayden's death, Hainburg, September 4, 1701, and of his widow's re-marriage, Hainburg, January 8, 1702.
Register of the composer's marriage, (St. Stephen's, Vienna, November 26, 1760).
The composer's signature (quittance for salary) Eisenstadt, January, 1762.
Register of Mathias Hayden's death, Rohrau, September 14, 1763, and the monument to him now in Rohrau Churchyard.
Frequent concert notices, both of the composer and his brother Michael, the latter at Salzburg.

APPENDICES. 97

                Habitual signature for many years of Michael Hayden.

                The composer's monument in Count Harrach's Park at Rohrau.

(c) *Haidin* : The name of the composer's mother is so given on the monument in Rohrau Churchyard.

(d) *Heyden:* The composer's name is so written throughout the " Convention und Verhaltungs-Norma " under which he held his appointment at Eisenstadt.

(e) *Heiden :* Register of Thomas Heiden's baptism, Hainburg, 1655.

(f) *Hayd'n :* } Occasionally, though rarely, in concert
(g) *Haydln :* } programmes.

(h) *Haydn :* Register of Mathias Haydn's baptism, Hainburg, January 31, 1699.

                The composer's habitual signature after February, 1762.

                Register of his wife's death, Baden, March 20, 1800.

                Diploma of the Freedom of Vienna, April 1, 1804.

                Many notices and concert programmes.

                Monument to the composer in the Einsiedeln Church at Eisenstadt.

A CROATIAN COMPOSER.

(*i*) *Haidn:*   Register of Barbara Haidn's baptism, Hainburg, January 2, 1658.
Frequent notices and concert programmes.
Letter of Beethoven, 1822.

(*k*) *Hayrn:*   Register of Thomas Hayrn's marriage, Hainburg, November 23, 1687—his father's name is also given as Caspar Hayrn; see letters (*a*), (*b*), and (*c*).

(*l*) *Hein:*   Register of Mathias Hein's marriage, Rohrau, November 24, 1728.

(*m*) *Haden:*
(*n*) *Hädn:*
(*o*) *Hayn:*   } Occasional variants in registers and documents at Hainburg, Rohrau, &c., noted by Dr. Pohl.
(*p*) *Hain:*
(*q*) *Heim:*

www.ingramcontent.com/pod-product-compliance
Lightning Source LLC
Chambersburg PA
CBHW021948160426
43195CB00011B/1271